Where Do
I Come From,
Daddy?

ISBN 979-8-89130-667-7 (paperback)
ISBN 979-8-89130-668-4 (digital)

Christian Faith Publishing
832 Park Avenue
Meadville, PA 16335
www.christianfaithpublishing.com

Printed in the United States of America

Where Do I Come From, Daddy?

James Ray

JAMESON. Daddy, where do I come from?

DAD. What do you mean, Jameson?

JAMESON. Like where do I come from, Daddy?

DAD. Well, Jameson, one night, about nine years ago, your mom and I were in Costa Rica on vacation, and your mom was having some adult drinks and…

JAMESON. No, no, no, Dad! I know that, Dad! They teach us in school about where babies come from. I mean, where did our families come from? Like where were you born and your mom and your dad and mommy's mom and papa?

DAD. Oh okay, sorry, Jameson, put some bait on your pole and cask it way out and have a seat, and I will tell you all about it...

Well, let's start with your mommy's side. Your great-grandparents named Carmen and Alfonso Rodriguez were born in Mexico, and they are the parents of your grandpa, Gerardo Rodriguez. Your other great-grandparents' names were Elias Gonzalez and Josefina Medina, and they were also born in Yuriria, Mexico, and they are the parents of your grandma, Eliva Rodriguez. Unfortunately, your great-grandma Josefina passed away when your grandma was six years old, so your great-great-grandma Yoya Elodia raised her.

DAD. Your great grandparents on my side of the family were Stanzer James Mosley and Algerlie Mosley, who are the parents of your grandma Shirley. Stanzer was born in Wewoka, Oklahoma, and Algerlie was born in Harris, Oklahoma. Your great-grandpa, Charles Ray, was born in Muskogee, Oklahoma, and Odetta Ray was born in Helena, Arkansas. They are the parents of your grandpa Gary Ray.

JAMESON. Wow, Daddy, my family is not even from Texas, so how did we get here?

DAD. Your grandpa Gerardo and your grandma Elvia both were born in Mexico. They wanted better opportunities for your mommy and your mommy's siblings, so Grandpa Gerardo journeyed to Chicago where he had family, and he worked and saved money for the wedding with your grandma Elvia. Once your grandma Elvia was able to come they moved to Arvin, California, where they established their life and still live now.

JAMESON. Oh, so that's how we got to California.

CALIFORNIA

ARVIN

DAD. Yes, Jameson, that is how your mommy was born in California.

JAMESON. Okay, Daddy, so how did your side of the family get to Cali?

DAD. Your great grandpa Charles Ray and great grandma Odetta Ray move to California from the south to look for better opportunities as well, and they settled in Bakersfield, California. So your grandma Shirley and your grandpa Gary were born in Bakersfield, California, and after they got married, they had a few of your uncles, then they got it right and had me and your favorite aunt Melissa. But before all these places, your great-great-great-great-grandparents came from West Africa.

CALIFORNIA

BAKERSFIELD

JAMESON. Wow, so my family is from West Africa; Yuriria, Mexico; Muskogee, Oklahoma; Chicago, Illinois; Bakersfield, California; and Arvin, California.

DAD. Yes, God has ways of bringing people together in unique ways, even when they live in different countries and cities.

JAMESON. Yes, that's crazy, Daddy! So if Papa Gerardo would have never left his family in Chicago because he loved Grandma Elvia so much and wanted her to be with her family in California, Mommy would have never met you, and you would have never made me?

DAD. Yes, when you put it like that, my son, yeah, I guess you're right.

JAMESON. So if Grandpa Charles would have never came to California from the south, then Papa Gary would have never met Grandma Shirley, and you would have never been born?

DAD. Yes, son, that sounds right.

JAMESON. I wonder how my story will be and where my wife's story will be.

DAD. Slow down, slow down, my son. Let's focus on that pre-algebra before you start thinking about your wife.

JAMESON. Okay, Daddy, I know, I was just thinking.

DAD. I understand, Jameson. Yes, son and life causes people to do things and move places, and you never know someone's story until you ask. I chose to move to Texas from California when you were born for a better life for you.

JAMESON. What about my brother Garrison? What's his story and why did you and Mommy have me seventeen years after Garrison?

DAD. Garrison, my beloved son, was born in Bakersfield, California, where Daddy was born. But he moved to East Coast to follow his dreams and play baseball after he graduated high school.

JAMESON. Daddy, why do you love Garrison and me so much?

DAD. Jameson, it's kinda hard to explain, but some day if you have children, maybe you can explain it to me. Life is interesting and taught me many things and that everyone has a story, Jameson, and you should never be mean or prejudge anyone for where they came from or their journey to where they are now. Life is full of ups and downs, lefts and rights, but always keep God first in your life and always do your best to treat people kindly.

JAMESON. How did you know all this about all these families, Daddy?

DAD. Well, I was curious about my family's stories, and like my son, I asked my family, and they told me.

JAMESON. Thanks for the talk, Daddy! I love hearing about our family and where we came from.

DAD. No problem, son. Let's get all our fishing gear and head home.

JAMESON. I want to dream about all the places my family has been.

DAD. Sounds like a good dream, my son, and if you like, we can start traveling the world to see where we came from.

DAD. Good night, my son.

JAMESON. Good night, Daddy.

About the Author

James Ray is a husband to his wife, Nancy, and father to sons, Garrison and Jameson. James enjoys traveling the world, experiencing new things, fishing, watching Garrison play baseball, and watching Jameson run around the house.